WHO IS CUTER?

Baby Quokka or Baby Pika?

by Mari Schuh

BLASTOFF! READERS 1

BLASTOFF! READERS, AN IMPRINT OF BELLWETHER MEDIA BY FLUTTERBEE

Blastoff! Readers are carefully developed by literacy experts to build reading stamina and move students toward fluency by combining standards-based content with developmentally appropriate text.

LEVELS

Level 1 provides the most support through repetition of high-frequency words, light text, predictable sentence patterns, and strong visual support.

Level 2 offers early readers a bit more challenge through varied sentences, increased text load, and text-supportive special features.

Level 3 advances early-fluent readers toward fluency through increased text load, less reliance on photos, advancing concepts, longer sentences, and more complex special features.

★ **Blastoff! Universe**

This edition first published in 2027 by Bellwether Media, Inc.

For information regarding permission, write to Bellwether Media, Inc., Attention: Permissions Department, 3500 American Blvd W, Suite 150, Bloomington, MN 55431.

Library of Congress Cataloging-in-Publication Data is available at www.loc.gov or upon request from the publisher.

ISBN: 9798898800253 (hardcover)
ISBN: 9798898801496 (ebook)

Editor: Rachael Barnes Designer: Jennifer Bowyer

Printed in the United States of America, North Mankato, MN.

Table of Contents

Kits and Joeys

Baby pikas
are called kits.
Baby quokkas
are called joeys.

kit
joey

Kits and joeys have round ears. Both babies are cute!

Legs and Tails

Joeys have thin tails.
Kits have tails too.
But fur hides their tails.

tail

Four short legs
help kits run.
Strong back legs
help joeys hop.

short
leg
back
leg

Ride and Hop

Joeys are born
one at a time.
Many kits are born
in small **litters**.

litter

Kits grow up in **burrows**. Joeys ride in mom's pouch. They peek out.

burrow
pouch

Joeys learn to climb and hop. Kits learn to run over big rocks!

hop

Kits often look **alert**. Joeys often look happy. Who is cuter?

Who Is Cuter?

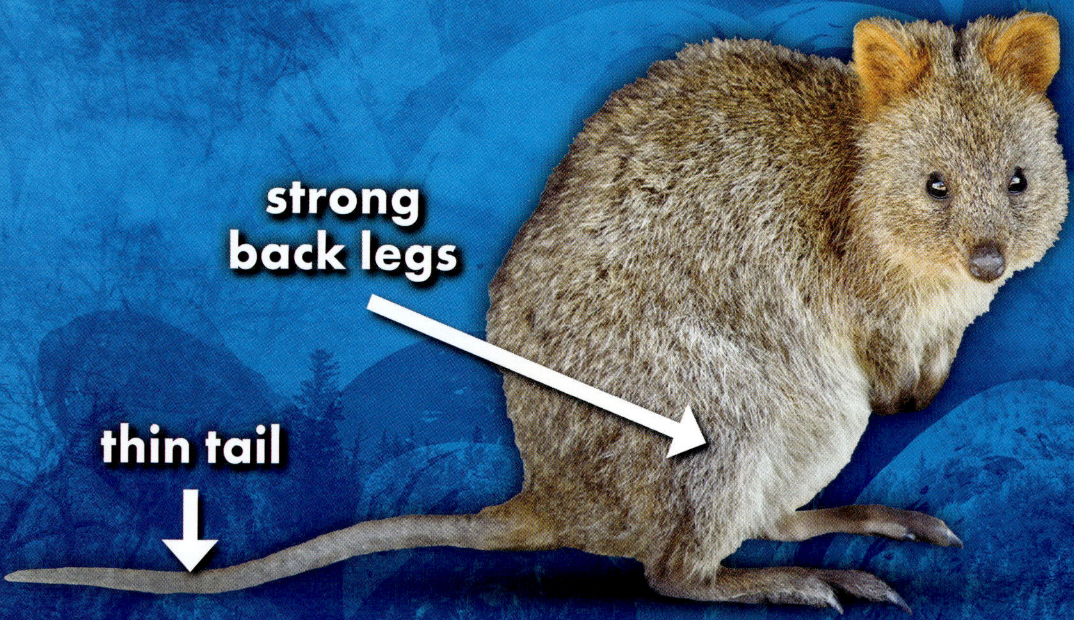

Baby Quokka

rides in mom's pouch

climbs and hops

often looks happy

Who is your pick?
Vote at
BellwetherMedia.com

Baby Pika

Glossary

alert

awake and ready

burrows

holes or tunnels in the ground used as animals' homes

litters

groups of baby animals born at the same time

To Learn More

AT THE LIBRARY

Jenner, Caryn. *Quokkas*. New York, N.Y.: DK, 2023.

Rocco, Hayley. *Hello, I'm a Quokka*. New York, N.Y.: G.P. Putnam's Sons, 2024.

Shaffer, Lindsay. *Pikas*. Minneapolis, Minn.: Bellwether Media, 2020.

ON THE WEB

FACTSURFER

Factsurfer.com gives you a safe, fun way to find more information.

1. Go to www.factsurfer.com.
2. Enter "baby quokka or baby pika" into the search box and click .
3. Select your book cover to see a list of related content.

Index

The images in this book are reproduced through the courtesy of: Damian Lugowski, front cover (quokka), pp. 18-19; Klara_Steffkova, front cover (pika); Eivor Kuchta, pp. 3 (quokka), 7; DLugowski/ Alamy, p. 3 (pika); Tony LePrieur Photography, pp. 4-5, 21 (often looks alert); fred.araujo.photographe, p. 5; Sara Petersson, pp. 6-7; Image Source Limited/ Alamy, pp. 8-9; Marie Henson, p. 9; Hideaki Edo/ Alamy, pp. 10-11, 20 (often looks happy); Victor.A, pp. 11, 21 (runs); Georgi Baird, pp. 12-13, 22 (litters); Louise Olifent, p. 13; JHVEPhoto, pp. 14-15; BirdImages, pp. 15, 21 (grows up in a burrow); Oleg Elagin, pp. 16-17, 19, 22 (alert); Kevin Schafer/ Minden Pictures, p. 17; photosbyash, p. 20 (quokka); EA Given, p. 20 (rides in mom's pouch); King Ropes Access, p. 20 (climbs and hops); Danita Delimont, p. 21 (pika); Nature Picture Library/ Alamy, p. 22 (burrows).